LITTLE CLIMATES

LITTLE CLIMATES

poems

L. A. JOHNSON

BULL★CITY
PRESS

DURHAM, NORTH CAROLINA

LITTLE CLIMATES

Published in the United States of America

Library of Congress Cataloging-in-Publication Data

Johnson, L. A.
Little Climates: poems / by L. A. Johnson
p.   cm.
ISBN-13: 978-1-4951-5769-1

Book design by F. H. Spock and Associates

Cover image:
Boyang Hou
Little Climates, 2017
Courtesy the artist
www.boyanghou.com

Published by
BULL CITY PRESS
1217 Odyssey Drive
Durham, NC 27713

www.BullCityPress.com

ACKNOWLEDGMENTS

The author would like to thank the editors of the following journals, in which these poems, sometimes in different forms, first appeared:

The Antioch Review: "Epistemology"

The Account: "Atlas" (as "Lull") and "Solstice"

The Carolina Quarterly: "Amniotic"

Cream City Review: "Forecast" (as "Prescience")

Day One: "Hush"

Devil's Lake: "Good Behavior" (as "Sclerotic")

Indiana Review: "Split-Level"

The Iowa Review: "Night Passage"

The Massachusetts Review: "Auroras"

Meridian: "Impermanence"

Nimrod International Journal: "Oarfish" and "Silvering"

Passages North: "Evaporation"

Phoebe: "Rare Geography"

The Southern Review: "Self-Portrait as Norway Spruce"

Yemassee: "Mutation"

CONTENTS

EPISTEMOLOGY

I never had quiet times in the kitchen
making an icebox cake.
I never inspected the back of the box,
folded wafers up with cream.

In the morning, you fix whatever
needs fixing. You make eggs
with toast. And in the afternoon, I walk
out far past the end of the acre.

Only then do the strays come
to the porch, looking for a dish of milk,
a can of fish left open. No arguing
or crying can be heard nearby.

In the evening, the walls confine
the regular angers. We listen
to the kettle sing on the stove
that nobody bothers to stop.

In the freezer, always, only the notion
of an icebox cake—its layers
softening to be like the real thing.
The icing, milk and smooth.

Stranger, if only things had been
a little different, I could be
old-fashioned in my happiness,
blushing and easy to love.

FORECAST

My ribs grow more inward by day. Each night,
I sleep with you in a small room, in which
we steadily, by each hour, suck up all the air.

I dreamt tonight of a glass-bottomed boat
floating through a pine forest, needles pierced
above and below my reflection in the lake surface.

We live in a house full of breakable things
and reassuring porcelain that we never touch.
Foxgloves with their toxic mouths open for us.

NIGHT PASSAGE

Mornings, I used to see in the bent grass
the shape of a bed, where one deer nestled down

at night. For a year I lived beside only an absence,
the ghostly depression of animal sleep.

Spring and his antlers lost tufts of fur, while my teeth
tried to grow in straight, wet monuments to precision.

After the error of alkaline blood, I kept myself
behind locked doors and learned to mummify my body

with blankets, preparing for the salt diet.
Later still, I saw the bed of the buck thinning, witch-grass

finally rising after so many months of tamping down—
his disappearance as unexplained as his arrival,

while my own presence became more silhouette
than solid. Between him and me, a sightless

understanding that existence could be willed
away at a whim, by rain or high wind.

FALL, BACKWARDS

I am the woman in profile, my face turned
half grey from the window, while outside

a dull geometry feigns a landscape.

Numbness releases from my sacral nerves.
I try to explain the science involved

to liquefy a silver powder on a spoon,

how precise information grows over a flame.
Compulsions arrive in glassine envelopes.

I was taught how to compress the incremental

just as a tourniquet stops convulsions.
Elsewhere, there is an interior with flowers—

thin poppies set out assuming in a glass,

a strip of light escapes into the dim room,
fragility and acquiescence are all that's left.

SHAPESHIFT

i.

Strange things click in the forest.
I feel the cold break in a tree hollow.
My body could be taken anywhere.

ii.

Beneath an indifferent grove, I stagger
and filmy minerals take hold inside
my lungs. Deer wake in the night air.

iii.

No one taught me the art of tracking:
how to construct piles of steering brush
to find an unclean kill; how to clean a kill.

iv.

In tall grass, velvet-colored antlers
loom above a curved spine collapsed
with fever, hooves splayed in the dirt.

v.

The dark mirrors in the lake water
and I confuse the liquid and the solid,
the shape and the shadow of the inexorable.

vi.

Under white pines, a fox tears at the carcass,
working his way down from the throat.
His hunger abides in my blood.

GOOD BEHAVIOR

Just past the winter-quiescent fields, the house
stood, lead paint peeling. The door opened

a crack, to let stale air in. We'd always assumed,
but we couldn't see much through the windows.

Instead we saw her hands, forked like claws,
and molded blankets shivered-white on the lawn.

Judgment in whispers kept us comfortable.
The neon sign for the Big 6 Market blinked on and off.

On good weekends, we danced a while,
kept our thin arms spaced at a proper distance.

What could I have known then of devotion,
lives not run out but ruinous, and all at once.

VANISHING POINT

In the thick of it, we couldn't see the end
of the road or the spotted body of a deer
curled up like a smoke ring that holds air

unnaturally long. I could tell you how roads
curve, play hide-and-seek with high beams.
I could tell you about pines and the American River

running parallel to us, icing over in late season.
All the while, with the minutes disappearing
the last of the cutthroat trout grow still

at the lake bottom. You could ask if his hands
were ready for swerving, if I would keep the seatbelt
cradled against my head. I could tell you how

after his brother died, he couldn't take much anymore,
cried in church and then stopped going to church.
Wore the same pair of jeans that whole year.

See now how the minutes seem longer, how the fog
should have been a warning. How we drove
and drove, convinced we would stop for nothing.

SHAPESHIFT

i.

Haze occludes the sunset
and I confuse the diffuse of orange
for the sun itself, danger with potential.

ii.

Lying in a field of wildflowers,
I fall asleep with wet hair. I dream
the names of stars, the myth of language.

iii.

Bats circle low in the air, cry
in the chimney. All evening I watch
their violent contours of longing.

iv.

A star shatters, the night expands.
Your weighted body, learned by heart.
In the without-light, I give of myself.

v.

My brain is only archive and flotsam,
my face willfully blank. Noiselessly,
I move into the dusty clearing.

vi.

Stars reveal their combustible selves.
Desire opens into a salt sail
under the smoke-filled sky.

PROVENANCE

High tides and yellow flags, signs warning us
of tsunamis, but we can't be cautioned,
too wonder-sick for what's below the highest

white caps. Your arm span severs the wind,
propels you effortlessly into the ocean. I wade
up to my knees, then drop in backwards, blind.

Necessity moves us underwater, while a nascent moon
whites the beach. We want to become invisible,
let our bodies drift soundless through the elements.

Beneath us, an empire of intense pressure
waits in darkness. Animal detritus softens
into sea snow, exposing the water columns down

to the ocean floor. Lower still, our only light is red.
Now transparent and defenseless, we swim deeper
to somewhere no human has ever seen. Water blocks

all hearing in our ears. It is July; it could be any season.

AMNIOTIC

From above, the seawall is bound
to a whiteness dividing meadow

from ocean. The air thins in late daylight.

Our brains evolved to identify patterns,
to find human faces in objects.

We regard the seawall together.

At this elevation, blood makes swollen
your finger joints, your fists rest

in your pockets. Fear is held away

by mere concrete. Eventually, distance
grows downward, making microclimates

in affection. A different language arrives

from detachment. The world separates into
two types of almost-sounds: a single small

voice and a silence, answering after.

HUSH

In these green hills, there's no longer time
for sleeping, for condolence notes.

Like a face, the sky looks back, with longing.

Another life, holding ice
in my mouth. Another life, leaving

my body out to be burned by the sun.

I had a lover once, with the eyes
of a monster, blue as a flood.

I felt the water lapping at my door.

I had a horse once, with the buck and gallop
of a stallion, that I led carefully

to graze on the cliffs above the Pacific.

༄

Twilight arrives and I tremble—

doubt sleeps among the stars,
tucked neatly into rows of twin beds.

This evening could go on forever,
like the plastic cord of a telephone

I used to wind around my wrist,

as I listened to your voice,
a miracle echoing out of the dark.

Tonight, I am witness to misshapen things,
the coast live oak growing coiled in our yard.

When the night decides, I won't see

them anymore, shielded by ghosts
and shadow. Only then do I want to stay

close to you, like animals in a wet field,
huddling awhile, saying each other's names.

AURORAS

The foam line of the lake breaks into ice.
I can feel the weight of a flood,

the granite of you sealing together.

Still, the lake water is all quiet, no smell
of rain. No sense of struggle or lungs folding.

Tiny algae float, stagnant. This is the illusion
of ice: stillness, suspension, possible safety.

Shrouded by my own veil, I never saw

the wet pearls appearing out of nothing.
Physics cannot explain midnight ideas,

how to close windows against water.

Today there should be no reason
for someone to drag the lake. No hooks

to use and put away. No delivery
of the polar news that we spend this life

following the most unworthy arrows.

TRANSMUTATION

Glass splits like a map. Say yes;
say the night is filled with torrents of red,
trouble, warm light; say thrill or chill.

In the Adobe Valley, early rabbitbrush
lines the freeway, we watch it burst into sight.

Out there, in the cold, wild horses
circle around each other to keep heat rising.

Hoof and fetlock, manes lengthening.
Unmastered, they will never know
the fidelity of a pasture, the lush emporium

of safety and grass to be found there.

Headfirst into the dark, I don't want
to want. Fire breaks in my face,
my lips turn to glass. What freedom

in that animal hunger for true north,
sugar and need. No maps, no getting-lost.

In this bedroom, a watery dress is removed
from the salt-depths of promise.

Lapse of a whisper, needles of light.
Bring cold into the room,
make a season out of breaking.

SOLSTICE

We bed down under the wrong moon,
beneath the cold cloud of memory.

In this repeating century, devotion

is measured with maps. I stack blocks
of glass to recreate my nativity.

ॐ

If invisible, I would curl up
among palm fronds, my body beading

against the green base like a drop
of rainwater. If invisible, I would sleep

in the desert's dry and wild opens.
If invisible, I would sink far down

near the bottom of a warm ocean—
to where only ashes float.

ॐ

Rapture pinks my brain. I want to forget
the weeks I trafficked in dim happiness,

folding in against your unshaved face.

In this lifetime, I see error in a hawk's flight,
the clear circles it makes in the air.

SELF-PORTRAIT AS NORWAY SPRUCE

I had been quiet once and for a long time:
turned my needles inward with discretion,
tolerated both birds and wild radishes.

When they came to possess me with twine
and metal, they counted, patiently, each limb.

Thirst overwhelmed me for the first time.
They took me horizontal, crushed belts

thick around my spine, forcing my muscles
to contract without labor. Veins cross-hatched
my monstrous body. The perfect discs

of my sapwood become exposed, revealing
a mien that is only one half of eternity.

I never had a mother or a child—
nothing to bind me to the earth but myself.

And when I become too thin to stand,
bring me to the knives, seal my mouth
with calla lilies, and call it a burial.

OARFISH

Rarely seen, they are washing up
on shorelines from Catalina to Santa Cruz.

Legend says the slime-covered, fatty beasts
mean bad luck, like the hundreds that beached

themselves in Japan right before the tsunami.
On fault lines, houses twist imperceptibly,

bending wood frames away from rafters.
The structural distortion can be seen only

from the street. Aseismic creep cracks
sidewalks, bows curbs. The tectonic plates

shift, displace horizontally, slowly ripping
towns in two. Asbestos settles in the breaks.

There are always signs we chose not to see.
Sinister changes appear on the ocean floor,

like scissors left by accident in bed.
The last fish just rolled in to Oceanside,

mouth agape in the afternoon low tide.
I am its encountering schoolchild, surprised

to find both the monster and miracle.

MUTATION

Switchback by switchback, we are driving in the night,
towards the top of Mount Diablo. Fog descends under

the barbed wire of crossed branches. There is sickness
blooming in everyone we love; black flowers open

imperceptibly in their smallest organs. Darkness increases
with elevation and the car tires edge the crumbling road.

Pine trees, trunks a hundred feet below, are the only barriers
to stop us from rolling. You misjudged this border once:

flipped your old truck sideways, then you watched
as the bones of your arms dragged along the ground.

The inevitable lurks in me. Abnormal cells divide
with speed. I trust the accidental as a greater paradise.

ATLAS

Untouched as a spoon, I wake
to the sound of your breath locked

in your throat, like a fox
fallen to the bottom of a well.

All rituals abandoned, the sun comes
through the shades. In silence, I learn

the cartography of a fire burning.

༄

Somewhere, I can settle in a bed
that becomes an island, speaking

against the-night-that-always-ends.

Somewhere in California, water
evaporates from the salt ponds:

one becomes aquamarine, another
magenta. Torment in their division.

༄

If I read the letter one hundred times,

maybe then I'll believe: no more
looking at almond trees blooming

beside the freeway, no more
pillow talk whispered backwards.

A dream, the weight of silk. This guilt:
cloud-soft, blueblack, unforgetting.

IMPERMANENCE

I waited for you all evening in my little room.
When you came, I took you to the window

to show you my one gift of naming stars.

To get here, you rode a train that divided
fields of foxtails, ice freezing their roots.

The tallest ones were taller even than you.

You didn't attend to my quixotic joy;
instead, you looked into the house next door

where a woman slept on a beige lounger,

her rounded fingernails covering her face.
An orchid widowed on a shelf. Snow began

to fall, filling the eaves with white. What is
fidelity if not a decision against this life.

SILVERING

i.

There are rumors about silver—
hold it to a wound to lustrate infection;
drop it into a basin of water to purify;

ingest it to ward off evil or conceal
it in a meal to poison. We ascribe
miraculous properties to shiny objects.

ii.

There were once operations at nightfall
where someone curious could have seen
red crowning in the mountains.

If you had investigated then, you
would have seen a woman sleeping
on top of a glassy knife, for safety.

iii.

To make a mirror: combine chemicals
and sugar with heated silver and pour
the mixture over glass. If you are successful,

light will come. Now you know the secret
that the image you see of yourself
is made only of combustible things.

EVAPORATION

Strange pockmarks spread in the desert;
pink crosses appear like visions in the Mojave.

They were not prepared: a carton of eggs abandoned
in the dusty kitchen, brass lamp left on all day.

Grainy video left a three-year mystery.
Meanwhile, someone was on the move, wearing

a blonde wig, crossing into places with straightened wire,
training her body to be used like a weapon.

Identity grew encircled. Their bones were found
beside the freeway, strewn by scavenger animals.

Specialists were called to examine the drying parts
and fibrous knobs with expensive metal tools.

SPLIT-LEVEL

Today, the two of us perform a funeral for a home—
we wreathe the doorway with lilies, carry
our possessions above our heads like caskets.

We scatter the enviable parts of our lives
across the lawn: a radio, ceramic bowls, a sweater

that never fit. Strangers stop by to look
at all our things. They offer us lemonade
and quarters, each one dressed in black.

Then with hammers, we begin the destruction.
Afternoon sun exposes the fine particles
of wool and fiberglass that kept us warm.

Behind the medicine cabinet, we find razor blades
rusted in a wall-hollow. In the vacant lot next door,

a ravine appears in the dirt that no stray dog
will cross, wary of how far down it might go.
We know in some towns, this demolition is modest

or even ordinary. A bulldozer prepares elsewhere.
In a future, this house will become honeycomb
and bees will make clear honey out of all our mistakes.

CONTINUUM

The snow arrived too early—
a pair of deer caught
in a squall of white.

In another universe, mirror lovers.
Mirror mistakes, repeating
on loop. Why the sky is blue,

I used to know. I search
for endings in your soft palate,
clapper of a bell in your voice.

A forest waits slumberless for a groom
in black. Evergreen, I vow to be
fashioned of a first snowfall:

the kind that's quick-thawing, clear
without inclusions; a flurry
that nestles a house in silence.

Story with ice and curse.
Story with multiple endings.
Someday—after, after—

a pair of deer not caught
in a squall of white. Snow
that never arrived at all.

ABOUT THE AUTHOR

L. A. JOHNSON is from California. She received her MFA from Columbia University and is currently pursuing her PhD in literature and creative writing from the University of Southern California, where she is a Provost's Fellow. She has received scholarships and fellowships from Vermont Studio Center and Sewanee Writers' Conference. Her poems have recently appeared in *The American Poetry Review, Alaska Quarterly Review, The Iowa Review, Narrative Magazine, The Southern Review,* and other journals. Find her online at HTTP://WWW.LA-JOHNSON.COM.